FAVORITE
HORSE BREEDS

AMERICAN PAINT HORSES

by Cari Meister

AMICUS | AMICUS INK

Amicus High Interest and Amicus Ink are published by Amicus
P.O. Box 1329, Mankato, MN 56002
www.amicuspublishing.us

Library of Congress Cataloging-in-Publication Data
Names: Meister, Cari, author.
Title: American Paint horses / by Cari Meister.
Description: Mankato, Minnesota : Amicus, [2019] | Series: Favorite horse breeds | Audience: K to grade 3. | Includes bibliographical references and index.
Identifiers: LCCN 2017020396| ISBN 9781681514208 (library bound) | ISBN 9781681523408 (pbk.) | ISBN 9781681515021 (ebook)
Subjects: LCSH: American paint horse--Juvenile literature. | Horse breeds--Juvenile literature.
Classification: LCC SF293.A47 M45 2019 | DDC 636.1/3--dc23
LC record available at https://lccn.loc.gov/2017020396

Editor: Wendy Dieker
Designer: Veronica Scott
Photo Researcher: Holly Young

Printed in China

HC 10 9 8 7 6 5 4 3 2 1
PB 10 9 8 7 6 5 4 3 2 1

TABLE OF CONTENTS

FAST AND FLASHY

A horse runs in a barrel race. He is strong. He is fast. He is flashy. He has bold marks and bold moves. He is an American paint horse.

SPANISH ROOTS

Spanish explorers brought paint horses to America on boats. These horses mixed with wild horses. They mixed with other horses, too.

BRAVE AND BOLD

Native Americans loved paint horses. They liked how paints looked. But more importantly, paint horses were brave. They were good in battle.

A PAINT IS A PINTO

A **pinto** is any horse with spots. Almost all horses in the paint breed are pintos. But pinto is not a breed. Pinto is a color pattern. Not all pintos are American paint horses.

Did You Know?

Paint horses can have a solid coat, but not many do.

SPOT PATTERNS

Paint horses have three main spot patterns. This **tobiano** has white marks that tend to go from its back down to its feet. An **overo's** marks usually run along the horse's sides. A **tovero** is a mix of the other two patterns.

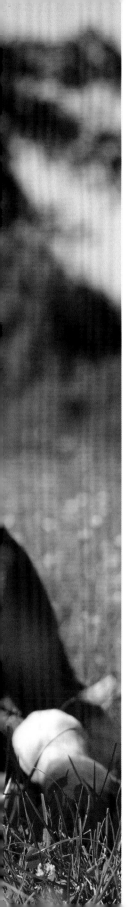

FOALS

Paint **foals** are born with their marks. Sometimes they match their parents. Like all foals, paint foals have long legs. They are almost as long as adult horse legs.

STRONG AND QUICK

Paint horses have thick chests. They have strong legs. They can turn quickly. They do well in **rodeo** events. They follow the rider's commands.

Did You Know?
Paints are good in the reining event. They stop quickly, walk backwards, and spin.

SMART AND HELPFUL

Paints are smart. They learn fast.

They are a big help on a ranch.

They help ranchers move cattle.

A trained paint horse knows

what to do.

CALM AND WILLING

Paint horses are calm. They do not scare easily. They are easy to ride on a trail. They are willing to obey their riders. Paints are easy horses to love.

HOW DO YOU KNOW IT'S AN AMERICAN PAINT HORSE?

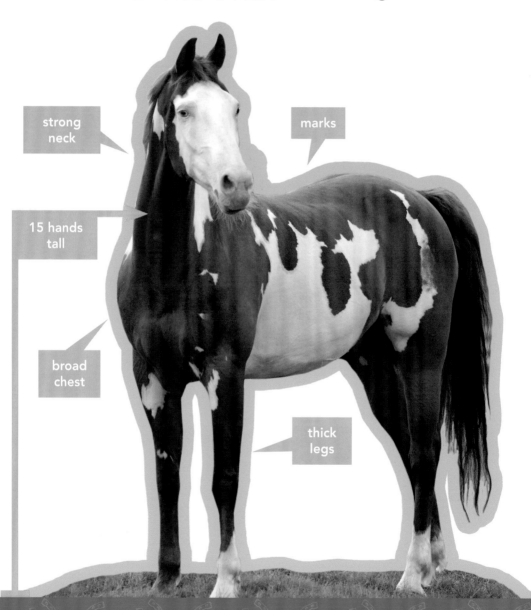

strong neck

marks

15 hands tall

broad chest

thick legs

WORDS TO KNOW

foal – a baby horse.

overo – a markings pattern that tends to be more horizontal; overos usually have dark legs, one tail color, and blue eyes.

pinto – any horse that has colored marks; it can be any breed.

reining – a Western rodeo event where horses are judged on how they move, turn, and stop.

rodeo – a Western horse competition where riders and horses show skills related to handling cattle.

tobiano – a markings pattern that tends to be vertical; tobianos usually have white legs, a dark face, and two colors in the tail.

tovero – a markings pattern that is a mix of tobiano and overo.

LEARN MORE

Books

Hansen, Grace. *American Paint Horses.* Minneapolis: Abdo Publishing, 2016.

Kolpin, Molly. *Favorite Horses: Breeds Girls Love.* Minneapolis: Capstone, 2015.

Websites

American Junior Paint Horse Association
http://apha.com/ajpha/

Horse | Kids, Cows & More
http://www.kidscowsandmore.org/horse/

INDEX